A2 **PE** for AQA
WORKBOOK

Nesta Wiggins-James • Rob James • Graham Thompson

www.heinemann.co.uk
✓ Free online support
✓ Useful weblinks
✓ 24 hour online ordering

01865 888058

Inspiring generations

Heinemann Educational Publishers
Halley Court, Jordan Hill, Oxford OX2 8EJ
Part of Harcourt Education

Heinemann is the registered trademark of
Harcourt Education Limited

© Harcourt 2006

First published 2006

11 10 09 08 07 06
10 9 8 7 6 5 4 3 2 1

British Library Cataloguing in Publication Data is available
from the British Library on request.

10-digit ISBN: 0 435 49941 6
13-digit ISBN: 978 0 435 49941 6

Typeset by 🖊 Tek-Art, Croydon, Surrey

Original illustrations © Harcourt Education Limited, 2006

Cover photo: © Alamy/Image State

Acknowledgements
Every effort has been made to contact copyright holders of material
reproduced in this book. Any omissions will be rectified in subsequent
printings if notice is given to the publishers.

AQA examination questions are reproduced courtesy of the Assessment and
Qualifications Alliance.

Contents

Unit 4: Physiological, biomechanical and psychological factors which optimise performance

Section 1: Physiological and biomechanical factors

Chapter 1: The physiology of skeletal muscle   1

Chapter 2: The sources and supply of energy in the body   4

Chapter 3: Factors that contribute to successful endurance performance   10

Chapter 4: Causes of fatigue and recovery from exercise   14

Chapter 5: Planning training regimes for elite performers   17

Chapter 6: Applying mechanics to sporting activity   22

Section 2: Psychological factors

Chapter 7: Personality   28

Chapter 8: Attitudes   32

Chapter 9: Aggression   34

Chapter 10: Achievement motivation   36

Chapter 11: Arousal   38

Chapter 12: Social facilitation   41

Chapter 13: Attribution theory   43

Chapter 14: Self-efficacy   45

Chapter 15: Group dynamics   47

Chapter 16: Leadership   50

Chapter 17: Stress and stress management   53

Unit 5: Factors affecting the nature and development of elite performance

Chapter 18: Talent identification and talent development   61

Chapter 19: Sport ethics, deviancy and the law   66

Chapter 20: The international perspective: World Games and the sport systems of the UK, USA and France   74

Introduction

This workbook is designed to support the information and activities provided in the student text Advanced PE for AQA. The content of the book is presented in a form that is identical to the AQA specification under the same sections and sub-headings.

Unit 4 (section 1): Physiological and biomechanical factors which optimise performance
Unit 4 (section 2): Psychological factors which optimise performance
Unit 5: Factors affecting the nature and development of elite performance
Unit 6: Analysis and critical evaluation of the factors which optimise performance.

The style of question contained within this workbook is varied, testing your ability to give definitions, apply knowledge to practical situations, respond to data and draw, label and interpret diagrams and graphs. Space is sometimes limited to make sure you plan your answer well, write concisely and use appropriate terminology throughout.

At the end of the workbook there will be some past paper questions for you to do together with some exemplar student responses and examiners comments to help you develop the crucial skill of examination technique.

Once completed this workbook should provide an excellent revision resource. Some of the main 'action words' used in this workbook are listed below. Take a few minutes to look over these now you know what you are required to do when answering the questions.

Command	What you are required to do.
List/Name	Short statements or single word answers are normally the requirement here. But be aware... if asked to list 3 factors THE FIRST THREE FACTORS THAT YOU LIST WILL NORMALLY BE TAKEN even if one of these are wrong and you have written a correct answer fourth on your list!
Describe	Give a description or an account of the main features. Say what you see!
Explain	Show understanding by giving reasons. One stage further than description!
Suggest	Use your existing knowledge to give a reason to support a statement or to use data provided in the question
Discuss	Use your knowledge and any evidence to form a BALANCED account
Plot	When asked to plot a graph it is expected that A PENCIL and graph paper will be used, fully labelled with calibrated axes. It is usually best to draw a line of best-fit through the points that you have plotted
Sketch	When asked to sketch a graph, exact plotted points (and therefore graph paper!) will not normally be necessary. However it will still be necessary to label the axes of your graph fully and with units!!

Unit 4: Physiological, biomechanical and psychological factors which optimise performance

Section 1: Physiological and biomechanical factors

Chapter 1: The physiology of skeletal muscle

1. Skeletal muscle has two main fibre types: slow twitch (Type 1) and fast twitch (Type 2). Fast twitch fibres can be further sub-divided into:

- fast oxidative glycolytic (type 2a)
- fast twitch glycolytic (type 2b).

Give two functional and two structural characteristics for each of the three types of muscle fibres.

a. Type 1   i. Functional characteristics

_____

ii. Structural characteristics

_____

b. Type 2a   i. Functional characteristics

_____

ii. Structural characteristics

_____

c. Type 2b   i. Functional characteristics

_____

ii. Structural characteristics

_____

2. In the table below place a tick (✓) in the box for those statements which apply to the most relevant fibre type.

Statement	Slow twitch (type 1)	Fast oxidative glycolytic (type 2a)	Fast twitch glycolytic (type 2b)
a. Fibres which have the lowest force of contraction			
b. Fibres which possess the greatest capillary density			
c. Fibres attached to the largest motor neuron			
d. Fibres with the greatest capacity to store muscle triglycerides			
e. Fibres with the greatest mitochondrial density			
f. Fibres with the poorest endurance capacity			
g. Fibres predominantly used by a 100m swimmer			
h. Fibres predominantly used by a shot putter			
i. Fibres predominantly used by a touring cyclist			

3. Place the following skills and activities on the continuum below which represent the predominant muscle fibre used whilst performing the selected action.

a. Maximum weight lift

b. Floor routine in gymnastics

c. Triple jump

d. Tennis serve

e. Iron man triathlon

f. 2000m Olympic rowing race

g. 1500m run

Type 1	Type 2a	Type 2b

4. Explain what you understand by the following terms.

Motor unit: _____

_____

_____

All or none law: _____

_____

_____

_____

5. Explain the pattern of motor unit recruitment for the following performers.

Cross-country skier: _____

_____

_____

A high jumper at take off: _____

_____

_____

6. Using practical examples explain how the synchronicity of motor unit recruitment can help a sports performer.

_____

_____

_____

_____

7. Using a sketched graph to illustrate your answer, explain how multiple unit summation can be used by performers to develop more powerful muscular contractions.

_____

_____

_____

_____

_____

_____

8. Explain how the muscle spindle apparatus operates in the quadriceps muscle group of a high jumper at take off.

_____

_____

_____

_____

_____

9. Following a period of weight training you notice an improvement in your 1 rep max score. What are the neuromuscular adaptations that account for these strength gains?

_____

_____

_____

_____

_____

_____

_____

_____

Chapter 2: The sources and supply of energy in the body

1. Give a definition of and units of measurement for energy.

Definition:

_____

_____

Units of measurement:

_____

2. In the space below draw a diagram that represents the following equation:

$$ATP + (ATPase) \longrightarrow ADP + Pi + Energy$$

3. Give an example of a sporting performer who predominantly relies upon each of the following fuels for ATP resynthesis.

Phosphocreatine:

_____

Glycogen:

_____

Glycogen and Triglycerides / Fatty Acids:

_____

4. In the space below write an equation that summarises the alactic or ATP-PC system.

5. Explain what you understand by the term 'coupled reaction'.

_____

_____

_____

6. a. In the space below draw a diagram that summarises the method of ATP resynthesis used by a 400m runner.

b. Write an equation that summarises this method of ATP resynthesis.

7. Fill in the missing labels in this diagrammatic representation of the aerobic pathway.

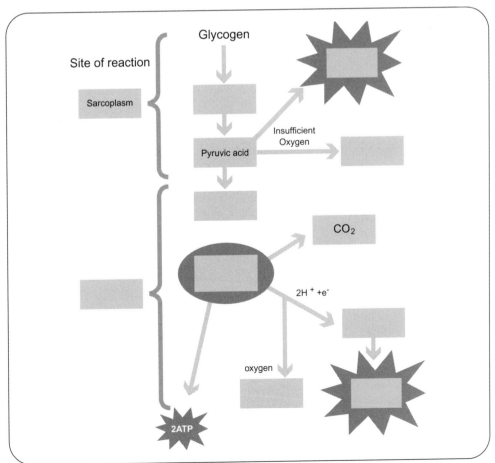

8. Use your knowledge of the energy systems to complete the table below with the relevant information.

Energy	Fuel used	Site of reaction	Active enzyme(s)	Molecules of ATP provided
a. ATP/PC				
b. Lactic acid				
c. Aerobic				

9. a. Explain what you understand by the term 'energy continuum'.

_____

_____

_____

b. In the space provided construct an 'energy continuum' with ATP splitting at one end and the aerobic pathway at the other.

c. On your continuum place the following skills and activities.

i.   an 800m run
ii. a squash rally
iii. a cover drive in cricket
iv. a downhill ski run

v.   a hammer throw
vi. a round of golf
vii. a 10K run

10. The chart below shows a possible energy profile of a netball centre during a match.

25% ATP/PC	50% LACTIC ACID	25% AEROBIC

In the space provided draw similar profiles for the following.

a. A 100m butterfly swimmer.

b. A 1500m runner.

c. An ice skater performing a routine.

d. A midfielder in football.

11. The table below shows the percentage contribution of aerobic and anaerobic respiratory processes to the total energy yield after different elapsed times during a run of 60 minutes' duration by a fit female athlete.

Respiratory process	Percentage of total energy yield at elapsed times						
	10 sec	1 min	2 min	4 min	10 min	30 min	60 min
% anaerobic	85	70	50	30	15	5	2
% aerobic	15	30	50	70	85	95	98

a. Draw a fully labelled graph showing the relationship between the elapsed time during exercise and the percentage of total energy produced by aerobic processes.

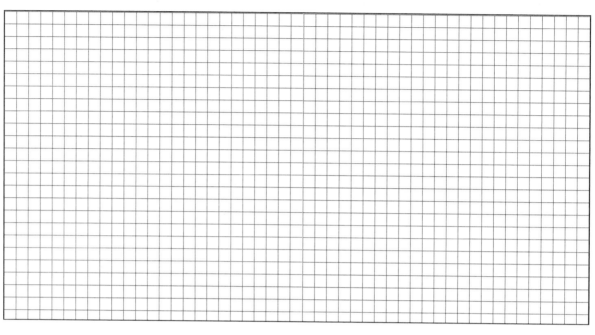

b. Calculate from the graph the relative contributions of the aerobic and anaerobic processes to the total energy produced after 3 minutes.

Aerobic:

_____

Anaerobic:

_____

c. Determine from the graph the time elapsed before aerobic sources account for 90% of the total energy yield.
Time elapsed:

_____

d. Briefly explain why the individual must rely on anaerobic respiration so much in the first 30 seconds of strenuous activity.

_____

_____

_____

_____

_____

_____

12. Complete the table below to identify two advantages and two limitations that each of the energy systems has to a sports performer.

	Advantages	Disadvantages
a. ATP-PC system	i. ii.	i. ii.
b. Lactic acid system	i. ii.	i. ii.
c. Aerobic system	i. ii.	i. ii.

Chapter 3: Factors that contribute to successful endurance performance

1. a. In the space below give a definition of Maximal Oxygen Uptake (VO2max).

_____

_____

b. State the units of measurement of Vo_2max in:
Relative terms

_____

Absolute terms

_____

2. Name three methods of measuring your Vo_2max.

i. _____

ii. _____

iii. _____

3. Identify and explain four factors that contribute to a performer's Vo_2max.

i. _____

_____

_____

ii. _____

_____

_____

iii. _____

_____

_____

iv. _____

_____

_____

4. a. Explain what you understand by the term OBLA.

_____

_____

b. At what concentration of blood lactate is OBLA thought to occur?

_____

5. A student takes part in the multi-stage fitness test.

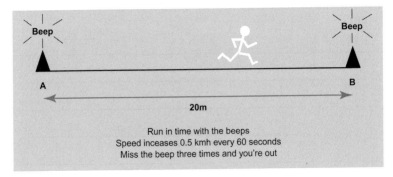

The table below illustrates the relationship between the concentration of blood lactate and exercise intensity (measured as the level achieved in the multi-stage fitness test).

Blood lactate (mmol/l)	Exercise intensity (level reached)
1	7
1.2	8
1.5	9
2.2	10
4.5	11
6.5	12
8.5	13

a. Using the data in the table, plot a graph to illustrate the relationship between blood lactate concentration and exercise intensity.

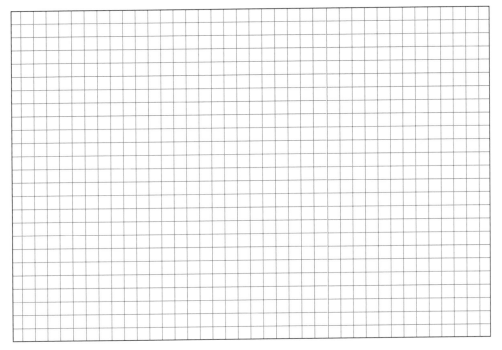

b. How would you use the data to explain that at level 7 most of the energy supply is from the aerobic system and at level 12 most of the energy supply is from anaerobic systems?

_____

_____

_____

_____

_____

_____

c. Mark on your graph the following.

    i. Lactate threshold

    ii. Onset of blood lactate accumulation

d. Suggest why the lactate threshold occurs below OBLA.

_____

_____

_____

_____

_____

_____

6. 65% of lactic acid produced is converted into carbon dioxide and water during the recovery process. State two different ways the body facilitates this conversion.

Method 1:

_____

_____

_____

_____

Method 2:

_____

_____

_____

_____

7. Other than conversion into carbon dioxide and water, state three other methods of lactic acid removal.

Method 1:

_____

Method 2:

_____

Method 3:

_____

8. What do you understand by the term 'buffering'?

_____

_____

_____

_____

_____

_____

_____

_____

Chapter 4: Causes of fatigue and recovery from exercise

1. Identify four factors that contribute to muscle fatigue.

i. _____

ii. _____

iii. _____

iv. _____

2. The table below reflects the heart rate of a swimmer who has completed a steady swim over 20 minutes followed by a 10 minute recovery period.

Exercise										
Time (min)	0	1	2	3	4	5	10	15	20	
Heart rate (bpm)	60	80	100	120	145	165	165	165	165	
Recovery										
Time (min)	21	22	23	24	25	26	27	28	29	30
Heart rate (bpm)	145	120	110	105	100	95	90	85	80	75

a. Use the figures to plot a graph of heart rate response during exercise and recovery.

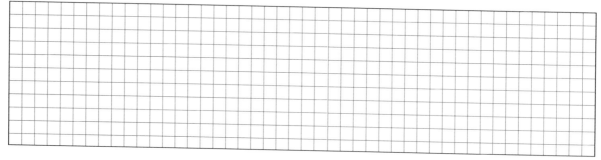

b. Explain the pattern of heart rate during the recovery period.

_____

_____

_____

_____

c. Explain the process of lactate conversion that takes place during recovery from the swim.

_____

_____

_____

_____

3. How could information on fast and slow components of EPOC aid a games performer in the following two instances?

During a match

_____

_____

_____

_____

Immediately following a match

_____

_____

_____

_____

4. The figure below shows the relationship between oxygen consumption, and time before, during and after high intensity exercise.

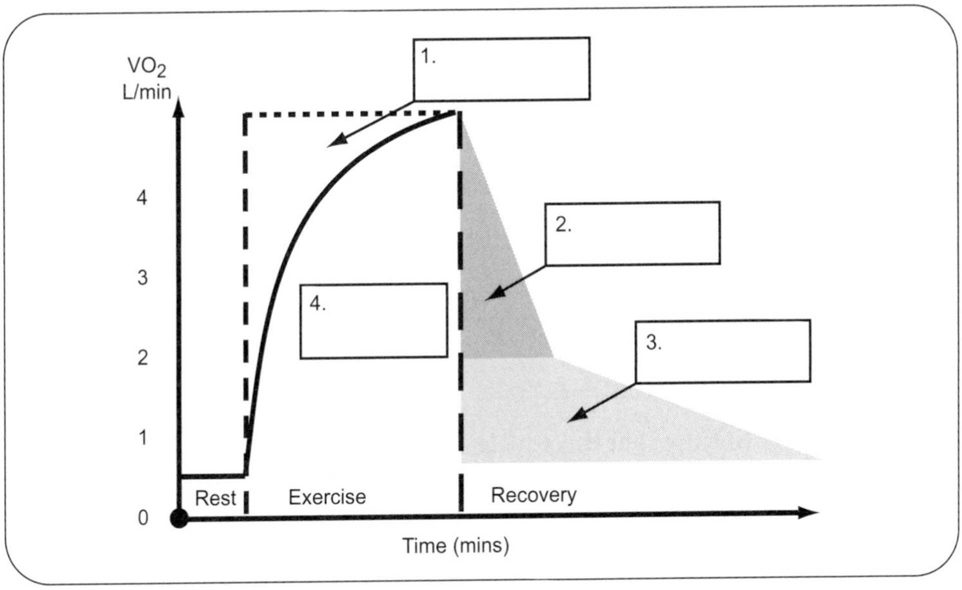

a. Label boxes 1–4 on the graph.
b. Briefly outline a cool down and explain how it could help to speed up lactate removal.

_____

_____

_____

_____

_____

_____

5. An athlete performs an interval training session. The table below shows the rate at which her muscular stores of creatine phosphate are restored during the resting intervals.

Recovery time (secs)	Creatine phosphate restored (%)
10	10
20	30
30	50
60	75
90	87
120	93
150	97
180	99
210	100

a. Using the table above, plot a graph of the percentage restoration of muscle creatine phosphate against time in seconds.

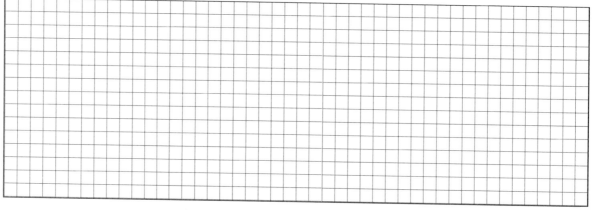

b. How can you surmise that the athlete is working at intervals of 80–100m?

_____

_____

_____

c. During a sprint interval training session full recovery is often advised.

i. On your graph show the effect of starting a second work interval after 30 seconds.

ii. Approximately how long will the stores last during this second exercise interval?

_____

_____

_____

Chapter 5: Planning training regimes for elite performers

1. The acronym SPORT FIT WIMP can be used to help you remember the principles of training. Explain how each of these principles of training can be used when designing a training programme for a marathon runner.

Principle of training	Application in the design of a training programme for a marathon runner
Specificity	
Progression	
Overload	
Reversibility	
Tedium	
Frequency	
Intensity	
Time	
Warm up/cool down	
Individuality	
Moderation	
Periodisation	

2. a. Complete the table below by stating whether the method of training suggested is appropriate for the performer identified. Write True or False in the column and justify your answer. The first performer has been completed to help you on your way!

Performer	Method of training	True / False	Justification of your answer
i. Weight lifter	Continuous training	False	Continuous training is primarily used to develop the aerobic energy system. A weightlifter requires an efficient ATP/PCr system. The best way to develop this is by weight training at 90–100% of 1 Rep-max.
ii. 200m swimmer	Interval training		
iii. Gymnast	Proprioceptive neuromuscular facilitation (PNF)		
iv. Marathon runner	Weight training @ 85% 1 Rep Max		
v. Hockey player	Fartlek		

b. Explain how PNF helps to improve flexibility.

_____

_____

_____

_____

_____

_____

3. Complete the table below by giving an explanation of the expected short-term responses of the body to 45 minutes of aerobic training.

Aspect of the body	Explanation of the expected short-term response to 45 minutes of aerobic training
a. The heart	
b. Blood pressure	
c. Energy production	
d. Lactic acid production	
e. a-vO$_2$ diff	

4. Complete each of the boxes below to give a **comprehensive** guide to training for a 100m sprinter.

A training programme for a 100m sprinter

Principles of training applied:

Components of fitness tested:

Energy systems stressed:

Example training sessions:

Methods of training used:

Adaptive responses achieved:

5. Complete the periodised year below for the same 100m sprinter. For each mesocycle give specific targets, and for each microcycle give specific examples of training sessions you would prescribe.

Training phases	Mesocycles	Microcycles
Transition		
Competitive phase		
Preparatory phase		

Chapter 6: Applying mechanics to sporting activity

1. Complete the table below by placing a tick (✔) in the appropriate column to identify whether each of the quantities listed is a vector or scalar quantity.

Quantity	Vector (✔)	Scalar (✔)
a. Inertia		
b. Acceleration		
c. Mass		
d. Speed		
e. Displacement		
f. Momentum		
g. Weight		
h. Velocity		
i. Distance		

2. For each of the quantities identified below, give a related equation and the specific units of measurement.

Quantity	Equation	Units of measurement
a. Force		
b. Momentum		
c. Velocity		
d. Acceleration		
e. Speed		

3. The table below shows the speed that an A-level female student achieves whilst performing a 200m sprint during her final practical assessment.

Speed (ms-¹)	Time (secs)
0.0	0
5.0	1
7.1	2
7.8	3
8.0	4
8.1	5
8.1	7
8.0	8
7.9	10
7.8	13
7.7	18
7.6	22
7.5	27

a. Use information from the table to plot a graph of speed against time during the sprint.

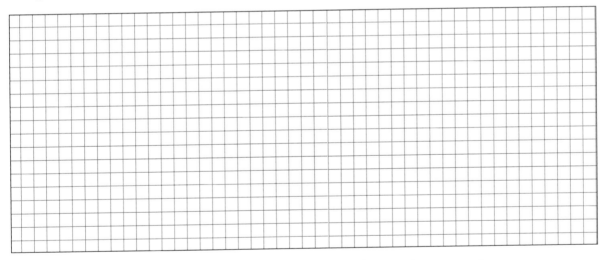

b. Mark on your graph the point at which the student reaches maximum speed.

c. State what happens to the student's speed between 8 and 27 seconds.

_____

_____

d. Use your graph to establish her speed at 1.5 seconds and 3.5 seconds.

1.5 sec:

_____

3.5 sec:

_____

e. Calculate her average acceleration between 1.5 and 3.5 seconds. Show all your workings.

f. The student's mass is 60kg. Calculate the forward force acting on her during 1.5 and 3.5 seconds. Show all your workings.

g. What is the nature of this force?

_____

4. Complete the table below to apply each of Newton's three laws of motion to the situation described.

Law of...	States that...	Applied to an athlete at the start of a 100m sprint	Applied to a push pass in hockey
a.			
b.			
c.			

5. On the free body diagrams below add arrows to identify the relevant horizontal and vertical forces that are in operation. (Hint: you must consider the relative magnitude (size) and direction of the forces.)

A: A sprinter accelerating out of the blocks.

B: A gymnast performing a handstand.

C: A 400m runner decelerating due to the effects of lactic acid.

D: A basketball player performing a jump shot.

A

B

C

D

6. The graph below shows the amount of force applied to a rugby ball during a conversion.

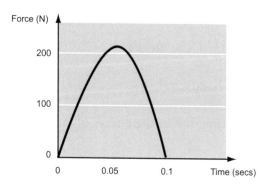

a. Give a definition of the term 'impulse'.

_____

_____

b. Using information from the graph, estimate the amount of impulse that acts on the rugby ball during the execution of the conversion. Show any workings.

_____

_____

_____

_____

c. The ball has a mass of 500g. Calculate the outgoing velocity of the ball. Show all your workings.

7. The graph below shows the expected flight paths of a shot, a badminton shuttlecock and a tennis ball hit with back spin.

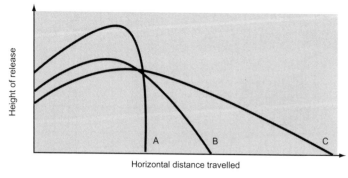

a. Which line – A, B or C – is most likely to represent that of a shot? _____
b. Explain your answer.

_____

_____

_____

c. On the diagrams below, draw the forces acting upon a shot and a shuttlecock immediately after they have been released.

i. A shot.

ii. A shuttlecock.

d. What factors determine the horizontal distance travelled by the shot?

_____

_____

_____

8. With reference to the diagram of a swimmer below, explain how knowledge of the moment of inertia can help the technique of the arm action in front crawl.

_____

_____

_____

_____

_____

_____

_____

_____

Section 2: Psychological factors

Chapter 7: Personality

1. a. Complete the following terms, then use them to label the diagram below outlining personality.

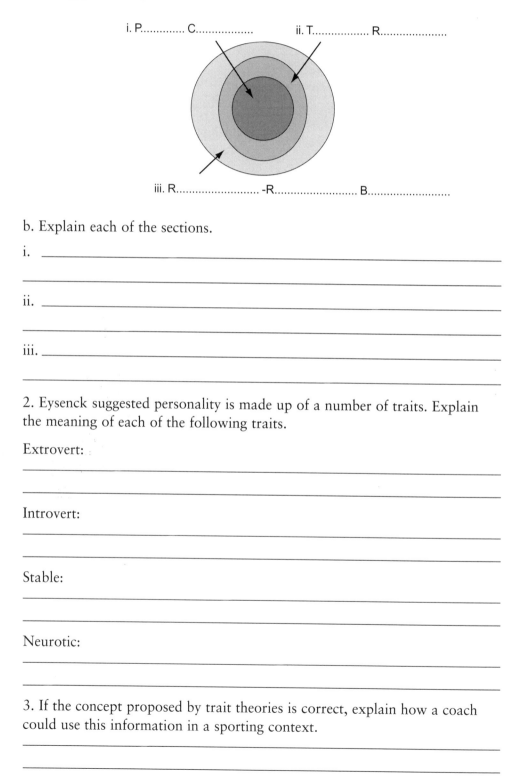

i. P............ C................

ii. T................ R....................

iii. R......................... -R......................... B.........................

b. Explain each of the sections.

i. _____

_____

ii. _____

_____

iii. _____

_____

2. Eysenck suggested personality is made up of a number of traits. Explain the meaning of each of the following traits.

Extrovert: _____

_____

Introvert: _____

_____

Stable: _____

_____

Neurotic: _____

_____

3. If the concept proposed by trait theories is correct, explain how a coach could use this information in a sporting context.

_____

_____

_____

_____

4. a. On the grid below place a cross to show your personality type.

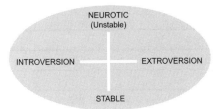

b. i. Complete the Eysenck Personality Inventory (EPI) below. Answer each question either 'Yes' or 'No'.

		Yes	No
1	Do you often long for excitement?		
2	Do you often need understanding friends to cheer you up?		
3	Are you carefree?		
4	Do you find it hard to take 'No' for an answer?		
5	Do you stop to think things over before doing anything?		
6	If you say you will do something do you always keep your promise, no matter how inconvenient it might be to do so?		
7	Does your mood often go up and down?		
8	Do you generally do things quickly without stopping to think?		
9	Do you ever feel 'just miserable' for no good reason?		
10	Would you do anything for a dare?		
11	Do you suddenly feel shy when you want to talk to an attractive stranger?		
12	Once in a while do you lose your temper and get angry?		
13	Do you often do things on the spur of the moment?		
14	Do you often worry about things you should not have said or done?		
15	Generally, do you prefer reading to meeting people?		
16	Are your feelings rather easily hurt?		
17	Do you like going out a lot?		
18	Do you occasionally have thoughts and ideas that you would not like other people to know about?		
19	Are you sometimes bubbling over with energy and sometimes very sluggish?		
20	Do you prefer to have a few but special friends?		
21	Do you daydream a lot?		
22	When people shout at you do you shout back?		
23	Are you troubled by feelings of guilt?		
24	Are all your habits good and desirable ones?		
25	Can you usually let yourself go and enjoy yourself a lot at a lively party?		
26	Would you call yourself tense or highly strung?		
27	Do other people think of you as being lively?		
28	After you have done something important, do you often come away feeling you could have done better?		
29	Are you mostly quiet when you are with other people?		
30	Do you sometimes gossip?		
31	Do ideas run through your head so that you cannot sleep?		

		Yes	No
32	If there is something you want to know about, would you rather look it up in a book than talk to someone about it?		
33	Do you get palpitations or jumping in your heart?		
34	Do you like the kind of work that you need to pay close attention to?		
35	Do you get attacks of shaking or trembling?		
36	Would you always declare everything at customs, even if you knew that you could never be found out?		
37	Do you hate being in a crowd who play jokes on one another?		
38	Are you an irritable person?		
39	Do you like doing things in which you have to act quickly?		
40	Do you worry about awful things that may happen?		
41	Are you slow and unhurried in the way you move?		
42	Have you ever been late for an appointment or work?		
43	Do you have nightmares?		
44	Do you like talking to people so much that you never miss a chance of talking to a stranger?		
45	Are you troubled by aches and pains?		
46	Would you be unhappy if you could not see lots of people most of the time?		
47	Would you call yourself a nervous person?		
48	Of all the people you know are there some who you definitely do not like?		
49	Would you say you were fairly self-confident?		
50	Are you easily hurt when people find fault with you or your work?		
51	Do you find it hard to really enjoy yourself at a lively party?		
52	Are you troubled by feelings of inferiority?		
53	Can you easily get some life into a party?		
54	Do you sometimes talk about things you know nothing about?		
55	Do you worry about your health?		
56	Do you like playing pranks on others?		

c. Follow the instructions below to assess you answers.

> *Obtain a score for Extrovert–Introvert dimension (E)*
> - Point for answering 'yes' to questions 1, 3, 17, 39, 44, 46, 49 and 53
> - Point for answering 'no' to questions 15, 29, 32, 41 and 51
>
> *Obtain a score for the Neurotic–Stable dimension (N)*
> - Point for answering 'yes' to questions 19, 35 and 55
>
> *Obtain a Lie score (L)*
> - Point for answering 'yes' to questions 6 and 24
> - Point for answering 'no' to questions 42 and 52

If your 'lie' score is 3 or 4 your answers for the test will not be valid. Look at those questions again and think why this might be the case.

d. Plot your results on the graph above. Compare the original assessment of your personality to the results gained after the test.

5. Outline two weaknesses of the trait theory of personality.

i. _____

_____

ii. _____

_____

6. Name the meaning of the abbreviations in the following equation linked to the Interactionist theory of personality: $B = f (P.E.)$

a. B = _____   b. f = _____

c. P = _____   d. E = _____

7. How does the Interactionist theory of personality differ to the trait approach?

_____

_____

_____

8. Name three methods to measure personality and evaluate the effectiveness of each.

Method	Evaluation

9. In the space below, draw and label a graph illustrating the Profile of Mood States (POMS) or Iceberg Profile.

Chapter 8: Attitudes

1. Explain the term 'attitude'.

_____

_____

_____

2. Name and outline the three components of the triadic model.

i. _____

_____

ii. _____

_____

iii. _____

_____

3. List four factors that may contribute to the development of a person's attitude.

i. _____

ii. _____

iii. _____

iv. _____

4. Name and describe two methods of measuring attitude.

i. _____

_____

_____

_____

ii. _____

_____

_____

_____

5. Complete the blanks using the words in the bullet list.

- recipient
- high
- context
- persuasive
- status
- situation
- quality
- message
- communication

The attitude of an individual can be changed by _____ _____.
The effectiveness of this method depends on the _____ _____ of
the messenger, the _____ of the _____, the characteristics of the
_____ and the _____ or _____ in which the message is
being delivered.

6. Using cognitive dissonance theory, explain how the negative attitude of a
group of young people towards swimming may be altered. Use practical
examples to illustrate your answer.

_____

_____

_____

_____

_____

_____

_____

_____

_____

_____

_____

_____

Chapter 9: Aggression

1. List four characteristics of an aggressive act during a sporting performance.

i. _____

ii. _____

iii. _____

iv. _____

2. For each of the terms a, b and c below, find the appropriate description from the table. Match the term to its description by writing the correct letter in the empty column of the table.

    a. Hostile/ reactive aggression
    b. Instrumental aggression
    c. Assertive behaviour/ channelled aggression

	Form of aggression where the aim is to achieve a goal, and any injury which may be caused is incidental.
	The actions of the performer are within the laws of the game and are goal-directed, with no intention to harm another player.
	Form of behaviour directed towards the goal of harming or injuring another living being who is motivated to avoid such treatment.

3. Select a sport of your choice, then give two examples of an aggressive act and an assertive act.

Sport: _____

a. Aggressive act: i. _____ ii. _____

b. Assertive act: i. _____ ii. _____

4. In the table below, indicate whether the example is considered 'aggressive' or 'assertive' by writing the appropriate term in the empty column.

Example	Aggressive or assertive?
Two boxers fighting for a world title.	
An American footballer punches an opponent following a hard tackle.	
During a cricket match the fielders 'sledge' the batsman.	
A goalkeeper slides into an attacker during the save and accidentally cuts the attacker's leg with his boot studs.	
A tennis player swears at an official after a bad line-call.	
A rugby player 'handing off' an opponent.	
A runner hopes an opponent will become injured before the race.	
A footballer, after being fouled, kicks an opponent but misses.	
A basketball player drives for a lay-up and collides with an opponent after shooting.	
Two cyclists collide and crash during the final sprint for the line.	

5. Explain the differences between the Instinct theory of aggression and the Social Learning theory of aggression.

_____

_____

_____

_____

_____

_____

6. Draw a diagram to explain the Frustration–Aggression hypothesis. Complete it using a practical example of your choice.

7. Explain the similarities and differences between the Frustration–Aggression hypothesis and the Aggression Cue hypothesis.

_____

_____

_____

_____

_____

_____

8. List five strategies the coach of a team may use to reduce the aggressive behaviour of the players.

i. _____

ii. _____

iii. _____

iv. _____

v. _____

Chapter 10: Achievement motivation

1. Explain the theory of achievement motivation.

_____

_____

_____

2. For each of the following characteristics, place a tick (✔) in the appropriate column to show whether they reflect a need to achieve (n.Ach) personality or a need to avoid failure (n.Af) personality.

Characteristics	Need to achieve (n.Ach)	Need to avoid failure (n.Af)
A sense of pride and satisfaction from competing		
Quick completion of the task		
Optimistic		
Perseverance		
Attempts to avoid shame and humiliation		
Avoids situations with 50–50 chance of success		
Takes responsibility for his or her own actions		
Dislikes personal feedback		
Attributes performance to external factors		
Performance tends to deteriorate when being evaluated		
Welcomes feedback		
Confident		
Worries about failure		
Chooses tasks which are very easy or very hard		

3. The performer's level of achievement motivation will depend on three factors. Complete the blanks below.

i.   P _____

ii. P _____ of S _____

iii. I _____ V _____ of S _____

4. Explain the following formula: $(Ms - Maf) \times (Ps \times \{I - Ps\})$

Ms: _____

Maf: _____

Ps: _____

I: _____

5. Complete the following passage using the words in the bullet list.

- avoidance
- choice
- satisfaction
- easier
- approach
- self-esteem
- risks

Performers who have a higher motive to achieve (n.Ach) will tend to have
_____ behaviour patterns. They will be prepared to take _____
and rise to the challenge, gaining feelings of _____ from the task even
if it is difficult in nature. Those who have a higher motive to avoid failure
(n.Af) will have _____ behaviour, as they will tend to opt for the
_____ _____ or not even attempt the task, as they wish to
protect their _____.

6. Explain the following terms, then illustrate your answer with practical examples.

Term	Explanation	Examples
Outcome goal		
Task-orientated goal		

7. Outline five strategies a coach may use to develop approach behaviour.

i. _____

ii. _____

iii. _____

iv. _____

v. _____

Chapter 11: Arousal

1. Explain the term 'arousal'.

_____

_____

2. With reference to the Drive theory, what do the abbreviations mean in the following formula? P = f (H x D)

P:

_____

f:

_____

H:

_____

D:

_____

3. The graph below illustrates the relationship between arousal and performance according to the Drive Theory.

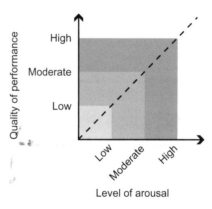

a. Outline how the performance of a novice and an experienced performer would differ according to their level of arousal.

_____

_____

_____

_____

_____

_____

b. Outline two weaknesses of this theory of arousal.

i. _____

_____

ii. _____

_____

4. Complete the following passage using the words in the bullet list.

- optimum
- deteriorate
- increase
- moderate

The Inverted U theory proposes that as arousal levels _____, so does the level of performance, but only up to an _____ point. This level is usually reached at _____ levels of arousal. After this point, further increases will cause the performance to _____.

5. List three factors which have to be considered when finding the optimum level of arousal for an individual performer.

i.   N _____ of the t _____.
ii. S _____ l _____ of the p _____.
iii. P _____ of the p _____.

6. a. Place the following activities in rank order of importance for high levels of arousal (where 1 is the highest and 10 the lowest).

Golf putt	
100-metre sprint	
Hockey penalty flick	
High jump	
Weight lifting	
Archery	
Pistol shooting	
Boxing	
Gymnastic vault	
Rugby	

b. Discuss your rank order with a partner.

7. a. What is the zone of optimal functioning and how can it help performance?

_____

_____

_____

_____

_____

b. Outline two weaknesses of this theory of arousal.

i. _____

_____

ii. _____

_____

8. The graph below illustrates the Catastrophe theory of arousal.

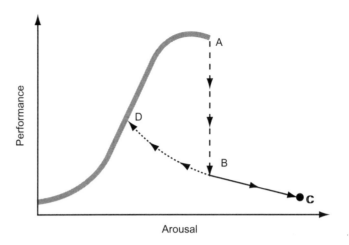

Identify the labels A, B, C and D. Then explain, using a practical example, the impact of each on performance.

A: _____

_____

_____

B: _____

_____

_____

C: _____

_____

_____

D: _____

_____

_____

9. Explain the terms 'attentional narrowing' and 'attentional wastage', and outline their effect on performance.

Attentional narrowing:

_____

_____

_____

Attentional wastage:

_____

_____

_____

Chapter 12: Social facilitation

1. Outline the concept of social facilitation.

_____

_____

2. What is the difference between social facilitation and social inhibition?

_____

_____

3. Zajonc suggested four categories of 'others' in his theory. Match the following definitions to the relevant term by writing them in the table below.

- audience   • co-actors   • competitive co-actors   • social reinforcers

Those in direct competition with the performer, e.g. another badminton player in a game.	
Those with a direct influence on the player, e.g. a coach.	
Those watching either as spectators at the event or at home via the different forms of media, including television, the radio or the Internet.	
Those performing the same task but not in direct competition, e.g. another player on a badminton court.	

4. Name the arousal theory associated with social facilitation.

_____

5. Explain the likely outcome of an audience on the performances of a novice and an experienced performer according to Zajonc's theory.

Novice: _____

_____

_____

Experienced performer: _____

_____

_____

6. What do you understand by the term 'evaluation apprehension'?

_____

_____

_____

7. List five factors which may influence the effect of social facilitation on the individual performer.

i. _____

ii. _____

iii. _____

iv. _____

v. _____

8. Outline the influence of a crowd with reference to the Distraction–Conflict Theory.

_____

_____

_____

9. List the advantages and disadvantages of playing a 'home' match in front of your own supporters.

Advantages	Disadvantages

10. Outline five strategies a coach could use to prevent social inhibition.

i. _____

ii. _____

iii. _____

iv. _____

v. _____

Chapter 13: Attribution theory

1. What are 'attributions'?

_____

_____

2. List three reasons why attributions must be used correctly.

i. _____

ii. _____

iii. _____

3. Complete the diagram below showing Weiner's Model of Attribution.

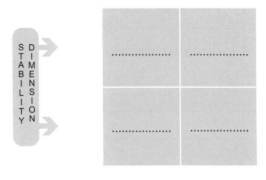

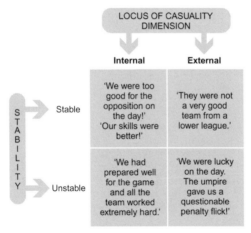

4. Give sporting examples for each of the categories named in the diagram above.

i. _____

_____

ii. _____

_____

iii. _____

_____

iv. _____

_____

5. Explain how the 'locus of control' can affect a performer's motivation.

_____

_____

_____

_____

6. What do you understand by the term 'self-serving bias'?

_____

_____

_____

_____

7. Outline the concept of attribution retraining.

_____

_____

_____

_____

Chapter 14: Self-efficacy

1. How does self-efficacy differ from self-confidence?

_____

_____

_____

_____

2. a. List six different sports in which you have participated.

i. _____   iv. _____

ii. _____   v. _____

iii. _____   vi. _____

b. Rank order them (with 1 being the highest) according to your personal level of self-efficacy.

i. _____   iv. _____

ii. _____   v. _____

iii. _____   vi. _____

c. Give reasons why you have a higher level of self-efficacy in the first two sports compared to the last two.

_____

_____

_____

_____

d. For your top ranked activity, list three specific situations in which you have high levels of self-efficacy. For each situation, explain why this is the case.

i. _____

_____

_____

ii. _____

_____

_____

iii. _____

_____

_____

3. Complete Bandura's model of self-efficacy shown below.

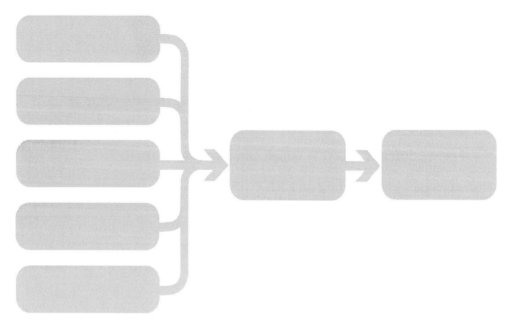

4. Outline five strategies a coach could use to develop high levels of self-efficacy. Use practical examples to illustrate your answers.

   i. _____

   ii. _____

   iii. _____

   iv. _____

   v. _____

5. Explain the following terms.

Learned helplessness: _____

_____

_____

_____

General learned helplessness: _____

_____

_____

_____

Specific learned helplessness: _____

_____

_____

_____

Chapter 15: Group dynamics

1. List four characteristics of a group.

i. _____

ii. _____

iii. _____

iv. _____

2. a. Complete the words in the first column of the table below, which outline the four stages of group formation as suggested by Tuckman.
b. In the second column of the table, explain the characteristics of each stage.

i. F _____	
ii. S _____	
iii. N _____	
iv. P _____	

3. Explain the term 'cohesion'.

_____

_____

4. a. Outline the meaning of the terms 'task cohesion' and 'social cohesion'.

Task cohesion: _____

_____

_____

Social cohesion: _____

_____

_____

b. Which type of cohesion is considered the most important? Give reasons to justify your answer.

_____

_____

_____

_____

5. Carron suggested various factors (antecedents) would contribute to the effectiveness of a group.

a. In the first column of the table, identify the antecedents as suggested by Carron.

b. In the second column of the table, give examples of each type of factor.

E ____ / s ____ f ____	
M ____ c ____	
L ____ s ____	
T ____ e ____	

c. Name two other factors which may affect the cohesiveness of a group.

i. _____

ii. _____

6. a. Fill in the blanks below for Steiner's formula for the effectiveness of a group.

A _____ P _____ = P _____ P _____

– Losses due to F _____ P _____

b. In the table below, explain each of the terms outlined in Steiner's formula.

i. A _____ P _____	
ii. P _____ P _____	
iii. F _____ P _____	1. 2.

c. Give practical examples to illustrate the cause of numbers 1 and 2 identified in the last row of the table above.

i. _____

ii. _____

7. List five strategies to develop cohesion and maximise the efficiency of a group.

i. _____

ii. _____

iii. _____

iv. _____

v. _____

8. Complete the following passage using the words in the bullet list below.

- Ringelmann effect
- co-ordination problems
- performance
- decreasing
- increases

As the group size _____ there is an increased likelihood of
_____ _____ occurring and the _____ of an
individual _____. This is known as the _____ _____.

9. Explain the term 'social loafing'.

_____

_____

_____

_____

10. Outline five methods a coach could use to reduce the effects of social loafing.

i. _____

ii. _____

iii. _____

iv. _____

v. _____

Chapter 16: Leadership

1. Explain the term 'leadership'.

_____

_____

2. List five characteristics of an effective leader.

i. _____

ii. _____

iii. _____

iv. _____

v. _____

3. Three main theories of leadership are shown in the table below. Briefly explain and evaluate each one.

Instinct theory	
Evaluation	
Social Learning theory	
Evaluation	
Interactionist theory	
Evaluation	

4. Leaders can be classed as 'prescribed' or 'emergent'. Explain the meaning of each term and give an example to illustrate your answer.

Prescribed leader: _____

_____

_____

_____

Emergent leader: _____

_____

_____

_____

5. The following leadership styles can be used depending on the situation.

- autocratic
- democratic
- laissez-faire

Match the style of leadership to the definitions below by writing them in the table.

This leader tends to leave the group members to their own devices, allowing them to make their own decisions and offering them little help with the decision-making process.	
This leader dictates to the group what actions to take, with very little or no input from group members in terms of decision-making.	
This leader encourages the group to discuss ideas and become involved in the decision-making process.	

6. Fiedler's contingency model of leadership depended on the 'favourableness' of the situation. List three factors which contributed to the 'favourableness'.

i. _____

ii. _____

iii. _____

7. Fiedler suggested two forms of leadership style. Complete the names of each below and outline when each should be used.

Type of leader	Used when situation is... (delete as required)	Situation characteristics (examples)
T_____-centred/ T_____-orientated/ A_____ leader	Highly favourable Moderately favourable Highly unfavourable	
R_____-centred/ P_____-orientated/ D_____ leader	Highly favourable Moderately favourable Highly unfavourable	

8. Chelladurai suggested that style of leadership dependa on a number of factors or antecedents. Explain each of the terms listed in the table below.

Antecedent	Explanation and examples
Situational characteristics	
Leader's characteristics	
Groups members' characteristics	
Required behaviour	
Actual behaviour	
Preferred behaviour	

9. For each of the following scenarios, complete the multi-dimensional model of leadership. How might the chosen leadership style differ to ensure group satisfaction?

a. Scenario 1: The instructor of a group of novice climbers attempting an abseil for the first time.

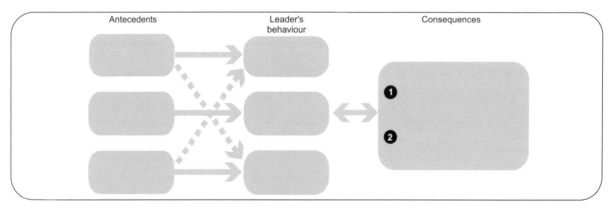

b. Scenario 2: The captain of an international team.

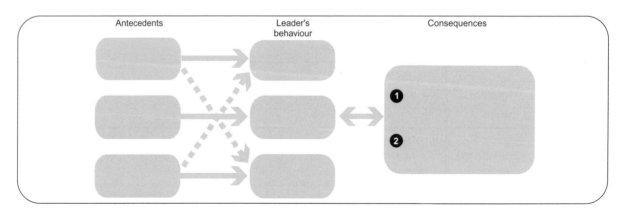

Chapter 17: Stress and stress management

1. Explain the following terms:

Stress: _____

_____

_____

Anxiety: _____

_____

_____

Eustress: _____

_____

_____

2. a. Identify the five stages of the stress response.

i. E_____ d_____

ii. P_____ of the e_____ d_____

iii.   S_____ r_____

iv. A_____ b_____

b. Describe each of the five stages identified above.

i. _____

_____

ii. _____

_____

iii. _____

_____

iv. _____

_____

v. _____

_____

3. List five possible stressors during a sporting situation.

i. _____

_____

ii. _____

_____

iii. _____

_____

iv. _____

_____

v. _____

_____

4. a. Identify the three stages of General Adaptation Syndrome.

i.   A_____ r_____
ii. R_____
iii. E_____

b. Outline each of the three stages identified above.

i.   _____

     _____

     _____

ii. _____

     _____

     _____

iii. _____

     _____

     _____

5. Explain the two forms of anxiety named below and give the characteristics of each.

Cognitive anxiety	Somatic anxiety
Explanation	Explanation
Characteristics	Characteristics

6. What is the difference between trait anxiety and state anxiety?

_____

_____

_____

_____

_____

_____

7. How does trait anxiety differ from competitive trait anxiety?

_____

_____

_____

_____

8. a. Identify the three methods that measure the stress levels of a performer.

i. O_____

ii. B_____

iii. S_____-r_____ q_____

b. Explain the methodology of each method.

i. _____

_____

_____

_____

ii. _____

_____

_____

_____

iii. _____

_____

_____

_____

9. a. Complete the Sport Competition Anxiety Test (SCAT) below.

Sport Competition Anxiety Test (SCAT)

Outlined below is a selection of statements related to an individual's feelings when he or she competes in sports and games. Read each statement and decide how often you feel this way when you compete. There are no right or wrong answers. Do not spend too long answering each question. Remember, choose the word that describes how you *usually* feel when competing in sports and games. Circle the appropriate letter using the following scale:

	Hardly ever – A	*Sometimes* – B	*Often* – C			
1.	Competing against others is socially enjoyable.		A	B	C
2.	Before I compete I feel uneasy.		A	B	C
3.	Before I compete I worry about not performing well.		A	B	C
4.	I am a good sportsperson when I compete.		A	B	C
5.	When I compete I worry about making mistakes.		A	B	C
6.	Before I compete I am calm.		A	B	C
7.	Setting a goal is important when competing.		A	B	C
8.	Before I compete I get a queasy feeling in my stomach.		A	B	C
9.	Just before competing I notice my heart beats faster than usual.		A	B	C
10.	I like to compete in games that demand considerable energy.		A	B	C
11.	Before I compete I feel relaxed.		A	B	C
12.	Before I compete I feel nervous.		A	B	C
13.	Team sports are more exciting than individual sports.		A	B	C
14.	I get nervous wanting to start the game.		A	B	C
15.	Before I compete I get uptight.		A	B	C

---

b. Score the test as follows to calculate your competitive trait anxiety.

- Questions 2, 3, 5, 8, 9, 12, 14 and 15: Score – A = 1, B = 2, C = 3
- Questions 6 and 11: Score – A = 3, B = 2, C = 1

Ignore all other questions.

c. Compare your findings with a partner and discuss the possible implications for performance. (Note: the higher your score the more likely you are to experience anxiety before a competition.)

10. a. Complete the Competitive State Anxiety Inventory – II (CSAI–II) below. Ideally, the questionnaire should ibe completed three times: first, some time before you participate in a competitive situation (for example, a school match); second, immediately prior to the start of the event; finally, after the event has finished.

Competitive State Anxiety Inventory – II (CSAI–II)

Outlined below is a selection of statements that athletes have used to describe their feelings before competition. Read each statement and decide how you feel at this moment. There are no right or wrong answers. Do not spend too long answering each question. Remember, choose the word that describes how you are *feeling now*. Circle the appropriate letter using the following scale:

Not at all – A   *Somewhat* – B   *Moderately* – C   *Very much so* – D

1.	I am concerned about this competition.	A	B	C	D
2.	I feel nervous.	A	B	C	D
3.	I have self-doubts.	A	B	C	D
4.	I feel jittery.	A	B	C	D
5.	I am concerned that I may not do as well in this competition as I should.	A	B	C	D
6.	My body feels tense.	A	B	C	D
7.	I am concerned about losing.	A	B	C	D
8.	I feel tense in my stomach.	A	B	C	D
9.	I am concerned about choking under pressure.	A	B	C	D
10.	My body feels relaxed.	A	B	C	D
11.	I am concerned about performing badly.	A	B	C	D
12.	My heart is racing.	A	B	C	D
13.	I am concerned about reaching my goal.	A	B	C	D
14.	I feel my stomach sinking.	A	B	C	D
15.	I am concerned others will be disappointed with my performance.	A	B	C	D
16.	My hands are clammy.	A	B	C	D
17.	I am concerned I won't be able to concentrate.	A	B	C	D
18.	My body feels tight.	A	B	C	D

b. Score the test as follows to calculate your competitive state anxiety levels.

- Question 10: Score – A = 4, B = 3, C = 2, D = 1
- All other questions score – A = 1, B = 2, C = 3, D = 4

The total of all even number scores gives your Somatic State Anxiety Score. The total of all odd number scores gives your Cognitive State Anxiety Score.

c. Discuss the findings in terms of how the cognitive and somatic aspects alter before, during and after the event. Also consider any relationship between your Competitive Trait Anxiety Score and your Competitive State Anxiety Scores.

11. a. Place each of the following stress management techniques into either the cognitive or somatic method column.

- Thought stopping
- Biofeedback
- Centering / breathing control
- Self-talk
- Imagery
- Progressive muscle relaxation technique

Cognitive methods	Somatic methods

b. Select two methods from each column and explain how a performer may use each technique to reduce levels of anxiety.

Cognitive techniques:

i. _____

_____

_____

_____

ii. _____

_____

_____

_____

Somatic techniques:

i. _____

_____

_____

_____

ii. _____

_____

_____

_____

12. Explain the following terms:

Goal setting:

_____

_____

_____

Outcome goal:

_____

_____

_____

Performance goal:

_____

_____

_____

13. You are the coach of a team. During the pre-season you decide to set both outcome and performance goals. For a sport of your choice, give examples of each type of goal which may be set for the team and individual performers.

Sport	Outcome goal	Performance goal
Individual		
Team		

14. a. Goals should be SMARTER. State what each letter stands for.

i.   S _____

ii. M _____

iii. A _____

iv. R _____

v.   T _____

vi. E _____

vii. R _____

b. Give an explanation of each aspect of SMARTER, illustrating your understanding with a practical example.

i. _____

_____

ii. _____

_____

iii. _____

_____

iv. _____

_____

v. _____

_____

vi. _____

_____

vii. _____

_____

15. a. Before your next competitive event, set yourself either an outcome goal or a performance goal. The goal must be SMARTER. For the next event set the other type of goal. Complete the chart below to describe the goals you have set.

Outcome goal	Performance goal
S	S
M	M
A	A
R	R
T	T
E	E
R	R

b. Discuss your results with a partner and evaluate which type of goal was the most effective for you.

Comments:

_____

_____

_____

_____

Unit 5 Factors affecting the nature and development of elite performance

Chapter 18: Talent identification and talent development

1. What is meant by the term 'elite sport'?

_____

_____

2. Give three advantages for the individual and for society when a society makes a decision to develop elite athletes.

Points for the suggestion	Points against the suggestion
i.	i.
ii.	ii.
iii.	iii.

3. Define the term 'talent identification'.

_____

_____

4. According to Oakley and Green, what 10 characteristics should an effective Elite Sport Development System contain?

i. _____   vi. _____

ii. _____   vii. _____

iii. _____   viii. _____

iv. _____   ix. _____

v. _____   x. _____

5. What strategies can a national governing body put in place to achieve a better talent identification programme?

_____

_____

_____

_____

6. Give three advantages and three disadvantages of systematic programmes for developing elite athletes.

Advantages	Society
i.	i.
ii.	ii.
iii.	iii.

7. What possible problems does the UK face in developing a modern-day system for the development of elite sport?

_____

_____

_____

_____

8. Name four major aims of UK Sport.

i. _____

ii. _____

iii. _____

iv. _____

9. What do the initials EIS stand for?

_____

10. What is the name of the organisation responsible for developing coaching in the UK?

_____

11. What challenges do national governing bodies face in the modern day?

_____

_____

_____

_____

12. Suggest five functions of the British Olympic Association.

i. _____

ii. _____

iii. _____

iv. _____

v. _____

13. Discuss the suggestion that elite athletes in receipt of National Lottery funding should be accountable for their results.

Points for the suggestion	Points against the suggestion

14. How could the government's high priority policy of PESSCLS (Physical Education and School Sports Club Links Strategy) aid in the development of an elite sport development system?

_____

_____

_____

_____

_____

15. Complete the table below to show:
a. the four components of the World Class Programme
b. the criteria for athletes for each component.

Components	Criteria
i.	i.
ii.	ii.
iii.	iii.
iv.	iv.

16. Give four characteristics of the organisation SportsAid.

i. _____

ii. _____

iii. _____

iv. _____

17. What criteria does an athlete have to meet to receive financial support from SportsAid?

_____

_____

_____

18. *Contemporary Sports Quiz.* Complete the gaps below.

a. One of the four home country Sport Councils:
S_____ E_____.

b. This has changed sports funding in the United Kingdom:
N_____ L_____.

c. Elite sport is at the apex of this: P_____ P_____.

d. Process by which children are encouraged to participate in the sports at which they are most likely to succeed: T_____ I_____.

e. The UK's system of sport is traditionally d_____.

f. The government Department for Sport in the UK:
D_____ of C_____, M_____ and S_____.

g. The UK's National Institute of Sport:
E_____ I_____ of S_____.

h. A comprehensive sports information service for coaches:
S_____ C_____ U_____.

i. Controls every aspect of their individual sport:
N_____ G_____ B_____.

j. Organisation responsible for the development of elite sport in the UK:
U_____ S_____.

19. *Task*: Research the website of a national governing body. Focus on its plans for the development of elite athletes.

20. *Revision blast*! Consider the factors outlined in the mind map below and add some relevant bullet points for each. Consider all the countries under study for a comprehensive revision approach to the topic of Talent Identification and Talent Development.

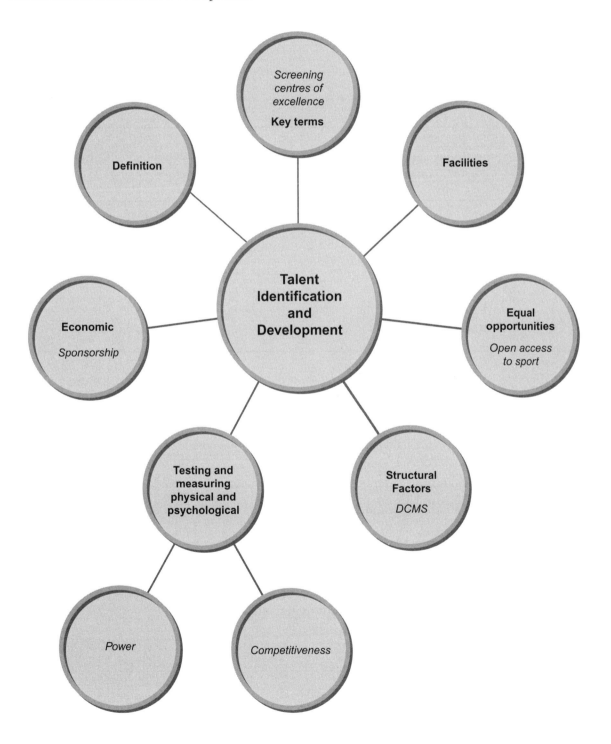

Chapter 19: Sport ethics, deviancy and the law

1. What is meant by the term 'contract to compete'?

_____

_____

2. Using a sport of your choice, give four examples of how the 'contract to compete' can be broken.

i. _____

ii. _____

iii. _____

iv. _____

3. Fill in the table below by giving bullet point information to summarise the three concepts.

Amateurism	Athleticism	Olympism

4. What are the common factors in each of the three concepts of amateurism, athleticism and olympism?

_____

_____

_____

5. a. What is the Lombardian ethic?

_____

_____

b. How does the Lombardian ethic differ from the three concepts of amateurism, athleticism and olympism?

_____

_____

6. What is meant by the term 'sportsmanship'?

_____

_____

7. Give reasons to justify that sportsmanship is still relevant today.

_____

_____

_____

_____

8. What is meant by the term 'professional sport'?

_____

_____

9. How does professional sport reflect the Lombardian ethic?

_____

_____

10. Why did professional sport attract the working classes in nineteenth-century England?

_____

_____

11. What are the advantages and disadvantages of a sport such as Rugby Football turning professional?

Advantages	Disadvantages

12. In the table below list the advantages and disadvantages of sponsorship to the performer and the sponsor.

Advantages of sponsorship to the performer	Advantages of sponsorship to the sponsor
Disadvantages of sponsorship to the performer	**Disadvantages of sponsorship to the sponsor**

13. How has the control of sport changed since the nineteenth century?

Control of sport in the nineteenth century	Control of sport in the twenty-first century

14. a. What is meant by the term 'deviancy'?

_____

_____

_____

b. Give four examples of deviancy from specific sports.

i. _____

ii. _____

iii. _____

iv. _____

15. How can conflict in sport be functional and dysfunctional?

Functional: _____

_____

_____

_____

Dysfunctional: _____

_____

_____

_____

16. In the chart below list:

a. the causes of football hooliganism
b. the strategies which clubs, security forces and local communities can implement in order to reduce hooliganism levels.

a. Causes of hooliganism	b. Strategies to reduce hooliganism

17. Illegal substances have been used for many years by sports performers. Name four different types of drugs used by sports performers and indicate in which sports they are most likely to be used.

Drug used by sports performers	Sports in which drug is most likely to be used
i.	
ii.	
iii.	
iv.	

18. Complete the chart below by listing the following.

a. Reasons why athletes take anabolic steroids.
b. Reasons against athletes taking anabolic steroids.
c. What strategies can be used to prevent athletes from taking anabolic steroids.

Reasons why athletes take anabolic steroids	Reasons against athletes taking anabolic steroids	Strategies used to prevent athletes taking anabolic steroids

19. *Match up!* For each term listed, find the appropriate description from the table below. Then match the term to its description by writing the correct letter (a–n) in the empty column of the table.

a. Sportsmanship
b. Deviance
c. Amateurism
d. Gamesmanship
e. Lombardian ethic
f. Professionalism
g. Olympism
h. Contract to compete

i. Commercial sport
j. Gentleman amateur
k. Endorsements
l. Shamateurism
m. Sponsorship
n. Ergogenic aid

Description	Term (a–n)
Bending the rules to gain an advantage.	
Participating in sport for monetary gain.	
Winning isn't the most important thing – it's the only thing.	
Behaviour that goes against society's general norms and values.	
To participate in sport for the love of it without monetary gain.	
Qualities that are displayed by a person or team that are highly regarded in sports such as fairness, generosity, observance of the rules and good humour on losing.	
All sport performers have entered into an unwritten mutual agreement to abide by the written and unwritten rules of a sporting activity.	
A philosophy of life exalting and combining in a balanced whole the qualities of body, will and mind; blending sport with culture and education.	
Under-the-table payments made to athletes who could not receive money from their sport.	
An emphasis on the principles of commerce with a focus on profit.	
The provision of funds or other forms of support to an individual or event for a commercial return.	
A substance or object that is used to enhance athletic performance. They can range from simple nasal strips to illegal drugs.	
Drawn from the upper classes and was regarded as having the qualities of refinement associated with a good family. Participated in the sport for the love of it.	
Where athletes display company names on their equipment, clothing and vehicles; the performers are contracted to publicly declare their support of a product.	

20. *The media, sponsorship and sport.* Consider the examples below.

a.

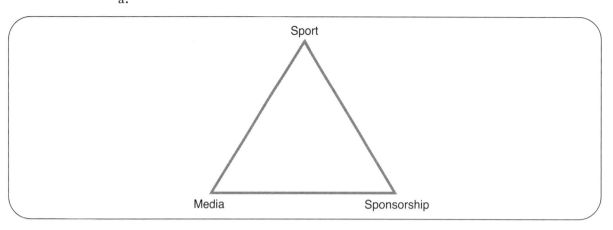

The golden triangle (Hargreaves).

b. 'Spectator sport and the media have fused together. The one is inconceivable without the other' (*Sport Britain 1945–2000*, Holt and Mason).

Examples a and b above illustrate the links that have been forged between high level sport, the media and the business world. Complete the diagram below by listing some of the positive and negative consequences the media has on sport.

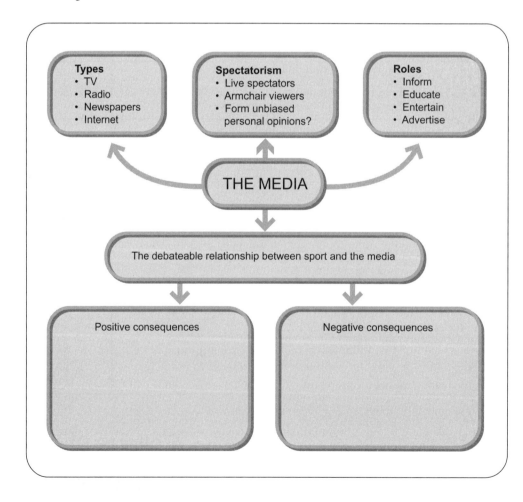

21. a. Do the following examples show gamesmanship (G), sportsmanship (S) or deviancy (D)?

i.   Stamping a player in rugby football: _____
ii.   'Walking' in cricket: _____
iii. Sledging in cricket: _____
iv.   Kicking a ball out in football when an opponent is injured: _____
v.   Taking anabolic steroids to win the 100m: _____
vi.   Bias in a referee: _____
vii. Coughing deliberately before your opponent tees off in golf: _____
viii. A player who is encouraged to play with an injury: _____
ix.   Owning up to a foul in hockey: _____
x.   Time wasting in football: _____

b. Discuss your judgements.

c. Give three other examples in the spaces provided.

i.   _____

ii.   _____

iii. _____

Chapter 20: The international perspective: World Games and the sport systems of the UK, USA and France

1. List in bullet point form the key characteristics of the UK, France and the USA, including aspects of their system of sport.

UK	USA	France

2. What is meant by the terms 'centralised' and 'decentralised'?

a. Centralised:

_____

_____

b. Decentralised:

_____

_____

3. Justify the statement 'The sport system in the USA is traditionally decentralised, apart from its preparation of Olympic athletes.'

_____

_____

_____

_____

4. How does the route taken by athletes to reach an elite level differ in the USA compared to France and the UK?

USA: _____

_____

France and UK: _____

_____

5. The statement by General de Gaulle for France – 'If we want medals we must pay for them' – is an example of a centralised policy. True or false?

_____

6. How can sport do the following?

Promote nationalism. _____

_____

_____

Be used as propaganda by governments. _____

_____

_____

Sustain social conflict or inequalities. _____

_____

_____

Be involved in political decisions. _____

_____

_____

7. What is meant by the terms 'capitalism', 'socialism' and 'mixed economy'?

Capitalism: _____

_____

_____

_____

Socialism: _____

_____

_____

_____

Mixed economy: _____

_____

_____

_____

8. How does professional sport reflect capitalism?

_____

_____

_____

_____

9. Why did France make a political decision to fund its elite athletes?

_____

_____

_____

_____

10. How are elite athletes funded in the UK, France and the USA?

UK	France	USA

11. Compare the following two National Institutes of Sport: the EIS (English Institute of Sport) and the INSEP (French National Institute for Sport).

Similarities	Differences

12. Why might countries specifically target certain sports in order to develop athletes from that sport to an elite level?

_____

_____

_____

_____

_____

13. 'School sport in the UK has *not* traditionally helped in the development of elite athletes.' Discuss this statement.

For	Against

14. What was the rationale of using the education system in the USA to develop elite athletes?

_____

_____

_____

15. Explain the role of the French 'section sport etudes' in the preparation of elite athletes.

_____

_____

_____

_____

16. a. What are the four dominant American sports?

i. _____

ii. _____

iii. _____

iv. _____

b. What common characteristics do they share?

_____

_____

_____

_____

_____

_____

_____

Women, ethnic minority and low socio-economic groups in relation to opportunities to reach an elite level.

17. What examples of racism and sexism exist in sport?

Racism	Sexism

18. Give three reasons for and three reasons against the suggestion that certain ethnic groups have a genetic advantage when it comes to excelling in sport.

a. For:

i. _____

ii. _____

iii. _____

b. Against:

i. _____

ii. _____

iii. _____

19. What is 'Title IX' and how does it influence sport in the USA?

_____

_____

_____

_____

The Olympic Games

20. What are the characteristics of World Games?

_____

_____

_____

_____

_____

_____

_____

_____

_____

_____

21. List the differences between amateur and professional World Games.

Professional	Amateur

22. Fill in the missing words.

Baron _____ established the modern Olympic Games in _____.
He was impressed with the ethos of a_____ and a_____ in
English public schools. He revived the _____ Olympic Games hoping
to create a sense of French n_____.

23. Outline the political controversies surrounding the Olympic Games
mentioned below.

Year	Political event
1936	
1968	
1972	
2000	

24. Give four reasons why cities decide to bid to host the Olympic Games.

i. _____

ii. _____

iii. _____

iv. _____

25. What are the objectives of Olympic Games marketing?

_____

_____

_____

_____

26. How has the role of women changed during the course of the modern Olympic Games?

_____

_____

_____

27. In small groups consider the issues outlined below and prepare a seminar session.

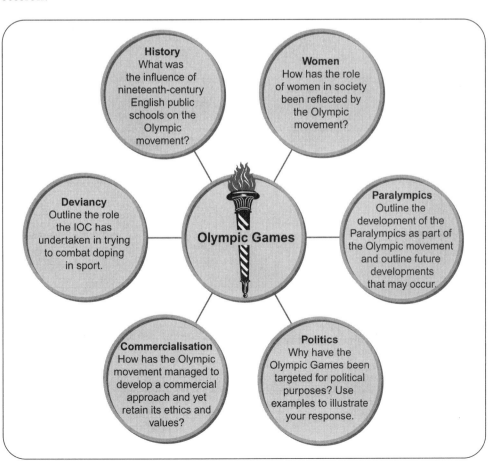

28. *Revision terms*. Fill in the second column of the table below by writing a definition for each term. Make sure you understand the relevance of the term to the systems of sport under study.

Term	Definition
Capitalism	
Federalism	
Collegiate sport	
Draft system	
Title IX	
The American Dream	
Lombardian ethic	
Centralised	
Nationalism	
General De Gaulle	
INSEP	
Decentralised	
Sport study sections	
Socialism	

29. Study the diagram below, which shows the organisations that have responsibility for the development of sport in the UK. In the blank boxes place some revision points for that specific organisation. Colour the boxes that are directly named on the specification.

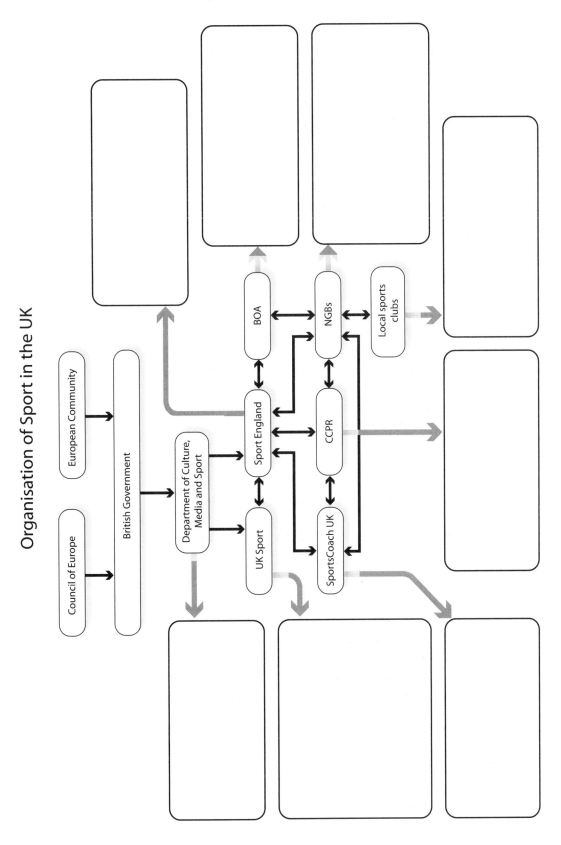

Organisation of Sport in the UK

- Council of Europe
- European Community
- British Government
- Department of Culture, Media and Sport
- Sport England
- UK Sport
- BOA
- CCPR
- SportsCoach UK
- NGBs
- Local sports clubs

Examination practice

Sample question

1. Elite performers will usually work with their coaches to produce a long-term structured training programme to improve their performance.

   a. In this context, what do you understand by the term *periodisation*?

   (3 marks)

   b. Describe **five** structural **and/or** physiological differences that you would expect to find between an elite athlete and a non-athlete, resulting from the effects of this training programme. **(5 marks)**

   Elite performers often use *goal setting* as part of their training programme.

   c. What value does *goal setting* have for the performer? **(2 marks)**

   d. Outline the factors that make *goal setting* effective. **(5 marks)**

(AQA January 2005)

Mark scheme

1. a. **3 marks** for 3 of:
      Dividing training into periods/sections for specific purpose;
      1. <u>Macrocycle</u> – long term plan of single year/between Olympics/world Championships;
      2. <u>Mesocycle</u> – monthly/weeks/period of training on particular aspect;
      3. <u>Microcycle</u> – weekly/days/individual training sessions to improve specific area.
      Or
      4. Training year divided into competitive phase/peaking/tapering/playing season;
      5. Involving preparation phase/pre-season training;
      6. Transition phase/active rest/out of season recovery.
         (Only credit if qualified)

   b. **5 marks** for 5 of:
      1. Cardiac hypertrophy/athletes heart/more muscle in wall of ventricle/increase in chamber size;
      2. Increased (resting) stroke volume/increased ejection fraction;
      3. Decreased resting heart rate/bradycardia;
      4. Increased blood volume/haemoglobin/red blood cells;
      5. Reduced exercising/maximal heart rate;
      6. VO_2 max increases/increase in maximal O_2 uptake/increased a- VO_2 diff:
      7. Increased stores of glycogen/triglycerides;
      8. Increased myoglobin content of muscle;
      9. Increased capilliarisation;
      10. Increased number and size of mitochondria;

11. Increased concentrations of oxidative enzymes;
12. Increased muscle stores of ATP PC/appropriate enzymes;
13. Increased glycolytic capacity;
14. Muscle hypertrophy;
15. Increased ability to recruit more motor units;
16. Increased lactate tolerance/clearance/delayed OBLA/Lactate threshold/high percentage of VO_2;
17. Decreased body fat;
18. Increase in bone density/ligament strength;
19. Increase in maximum cardiac output;
20. Reduced EPOC.

(N.B Accept opposites)

c. **2 marks** for 2 of:
   1. identifies future target/achievement/purpose/aims/objectives for the performer;
   2. In order to maintain or improve performance;
   3. Assists/aids motivation;
   4. Evaluation of progress/improvements.

d. **5 marks** for 5 of:
   1. Goals should be positive/looking to improve;
   2. Specific to the performer;
   3. Agreed between coach and performer;
   4. Formalised/written down/recorded;
   5. Seen by performer as being realistic/achievable;
   6. Goals must be seen as challenging by/to the performer;
   7. Expressed in quantitative terms/performance goals/explanation of how the goal is measurable;
   8. Using short/medium and long-term goals;
   9. Subject to appropriate revisions;
   10. Following evaluation;
   11. Requires feedback from coach;
   12. SMART/SMARTER/SCAMP.

Sample Answer (numbers in brackets refer to points on the mark scheme)

1. a. Periodisation is when you split the time available to train into different parts, improving different parts (1), improving different fitness levels and skills. It is normally done in a year. Pre-season training (6), during competition and recovery, i.e. pre-season working on improving fitness levels, during competition maintaining fitness and improving skill (5) and recovery, where you rest but still do some gentle exercise.

b. The physiological and structural differences are that the elite performer will have <u>hypertrophy of the cardiac muscle</u> (1) and therefore an increased cardiac output. They will also have <u>hypertrophy of the muscle fibres</u> (14), <u>increased capillarisation</u> (9) and therefore more efficient gaseous exchange. <u>Increased myoglobin stores</u> (8) and an <u>increase in the number of red blood cells</u> (4) and therefore haemoglobin makes the body more efficient for exercise.

c. Goal setting <u>increases the motivation levels</u> (3) and confidence (self efficacy) levels of a performer. This is because they are able to see what they need to work towards and what they have already achieved. It will hopefully <u>then increase performance</u> (2).

d. Factors which make goal setting effective are if the goal setting is specific, measurable, accepted, <u>recordable</u> (4), time phased, <u>exciting</u> (6) and <u>realistic</u> (5). They have to be related to what you want to achieve, able to measure them, <u>accepted by the coach and the performer</u> (3), given times by which certain goals should be completed and they also need to be achievable otherwise de-motivation may occur.

Examiner Comments

a. The student has achieved full marks for this part of the question. An explanation of the term 'periodisation' has been provided and different phases of the yearly cycle have been outlined and explained with reference to their purpose.

b. This is a good example of a concise answer which achieves full marks. Each of the differences uses the correct terminology and are not expanded making reference to the benefits of the physiological differences, as this is not asked for in the question. It is worth noting the mark for 'increased cardiac output' has not been awarded because the mark scheme specifically requires 'increased <u>maximum</u> cardiac output.'

c. Again another concise answer gaining full marks. The student has made two separate points with no interpretation required by the examiner.

d. Whilst the final section is credited with 4 out of 5 marks it is not the strongest answer. The student has listed the terms related to the commonly shortened acronym 'SMARTER', but not expanded fully. A very good answer would go beyond merely listing the terms and explain the principles of effective goal-setting and discuss types of goals which could be used.

Overall this is an excellent answer, using the correct technical terminology. It is written in a fluent and concise manner, with few grammatical errors. If the remainder of the examination paper were of a similar standard the student would achieve either 3 or 4 marks for their quality of written communication.

Examination practice – PED 5

Section A – Sample question

1. An individual must have a range of personal qualities and receive some external support to enable them to reach an elite level of performance.

   a. What personal qualities are necessary for an individual to progress towards an elite level of performance? **(4 marks)**

   b. Within the United Kingdom, what support or structures exist to help an individual develop to an elite level? Give examples to illustrate your answer. **(6 marks)**

   c. Schools and colleges often help talented individuals to progress to elite level. Discuss the similarities and differences between the United Kingdom and the United States of America in this respect. **(5 marks)**

(AQA June 2005)

Mark scheme

1. a. **4 marks** for 4 of:
   1. (Long term) commitment/self discipline;
   2. Determination/be the best/sets targets/vision/single minded/focussed/mental toughness;
   3. Motivation/Nach personality/desire to achieve;
   4. Self sacrifice;
   5. Resilience/ability to overcome failure/pass through pain barrier;
   6. Self-confidence/self efficacy;
   7. High levels of talent/natural ability;
   8. High levels of physical fitness/high VO2 max/equiv.

   b. **6 marks** for 6 of (max 4 per section): *Max 4 if support/structures only. Max 2 naming organisations only.*

   Example must be linked to specific structure/support. No marks for just naming an organisation. It must be qualified.

Examples	Structures & Support
NGB/Sport England/World Class programme/SportsAid/gifted & talented/aim higher/ Sponsorships/Scholarships	Financial support
set performance targets/ performance development plans	Support linked to success/world ranking
English Institute of Sport/ Sportscoach UK/UKSI/NGB's/ SportEngland/centres of excellence/academies/UK Sport	Network of elite or high quality coaching/Facilities

Continued

Examples	Structures & Support
English Institute of Sport/centres of excellence/NGB/ Higher Education	Sports science/technology/ nutrition/medicine/physiotherapy
NGB/ World Class Programme run by UK Sport/EIS regional scouts	Talent Identification Programme
Academies/Centres of Excellence/specialist schools/ colleges/county squads international development groups	Graded levels of competition/ Training elite groups

c. **5 marks** for 5 of (max 3 per section):

Similarities
1. Competitive sport is mostly extra-curricular;
2. Separation of PE and competitive sport;
3. Value given to the socialisation character-building characteristics of sport;
4. Recent initiatives in UK Sports Colleges (Centres of Excellence).
(Should refer to both countries)

Differences
In the USA: *(accept reverse answers)*
5. Colleges/Higher Ed nursery for elite/professional teams;
6. Large number of scholarships from school to college/uni/higher ed;
7. High level of competitive interest in school/college sport;
8. Use of high status sports coaches in schools/colleges;
9. Better facilities in USA schools;
10. High level of local community and school spectator interest in inter-school/college matches/more people watching;
11. High level of funding from local taxes/sponsorship/media receipts/gate receipts/commercialisation;
12. Less club development progression at grass root level.
(N.B Do not credit ethics/Lombardian)

Sample Answer (numbers in brackets refer to points on the mark scheme)

a. The personal qualities that an individual needs to progress to elite levels are; physiological they need <u>high levels of fitness</u> (8) in their chosen sport and a good training routine that they always stick to. Psychologically they need <u>good motivation</u> (3) to participate and the <u>ability to stay focussed if things go wrong</u> (5). Also good mental skills to concentrate in competition. They would also need the support of family and friends and good coaching.

b. The structures that exist to help an individual to develop into an elite performer are;

Out of school clubs. These clubs develop the skills that are taught in school.

<u>Satellite academies</u> (11) - are for clubs to set up for the <u>most gifted in their sport</u> (12) to develop their game even more, e.g. football academies run by premiership football clubs.

<u>Talent Identification</u> (10) - this is where scouts observe young players and see if they have the potential to become an elite player. These are <u>run by the governing body or scouts in each area of the country</u> (9).

<u>Specialist facilities</u> (6) - elite performers need good facilities to train and develop their skills. These are <u>provided by the English Institute of Sport</u> (5) and other centres of excellence.

c. The UK and the USA both help talented individuals to elite level although both have similarities and differences.

The similarities are that they both offer professional coaches to coach the talented individuals and they offer financial support and medical advice.

The differences are that <u>the USA helps players into major league clubs</u> (5). The colleges in the USA offer <u>scholarships for talented individuals</u> (6). The <u>UK has more of a club system than the USA</u> (12). Also in the USA schools and colleges have <u>excellent sports facilities</u> (9) and the teams are <u>taught by specialist coaches</u> rather than the PE teacher (8).

Examiner Comments

a. *The student has done well to sub-divide their answer into physiological and psychological differences, attempting to give it more structure. The key point to highlight is the distinction made with the higher level skills required to progress to elite. For example, 'high levels of fitness' and 'good motivation'. The latter part of the answer is too vague to be credited with marks and the reference to social factors is irrelevant in the context of the question, as it specifically requested 'personal qualities'.*

b. *Again this is a well structured answer, with clear sections for each point made. There is good use of relevant examples as requested. The organisations are correctly named and linked to the support they provide. A common mistake in this type of answer would be to merely list a number of organisations, which would not be credited.*

c. *The student has attempted to answer both aspects of the question, but not gained any marks for the 'similarities' section. The 'differences' aspect of the question is well answered, achieving full marks for the sub section. It is worth noting that even though enough answers are provided to gain marks for the total allocation, there is a sub maximum which has been reached. However, as good examination technique the student has provided additional answers which could have been given credit, if any earlier answers were incorrect.*

Section B – Sample question

Teams are successful because they combine highly skilled individuals into an effective group.

a. Successful teams are often said to be cohesive. What do we mean by *cohesion* **and** how may a coach help a team to become cohesive?

(4 marks)

b. Hockey is an example of an invasion team game. During a match, a midfield player will be running at differing speeds over a variety of distances.

Using examples, discuss the energy systems that would be dominant at specific times during a match **and** suggest the most appropriate form of training for this player. Give reasons to justify your selection of training method.

(8 marks)

Mark scheme

a. i 4 marks for 4 of (sub max 1 mark for explanation of cohesion):
   1. Cohesion – a tendency of a group to stay together to achieve certain objectives or outcomes/explain task and social cohesion;
   2. Show resistance to disruption.

How it is achieved *(Sub max 3 marks)*:

3. Establish common goals;
4. Particularly task oriented goals;
5. Ensure shared experiences/teamwork exercises;
6. Have highly motivated individuals/issue rewards/create desire for success;
7. Understanding and acceptance of individual role within team;
8. Utilise participative/democratic leadership/decision making style;
9. Keep team together/give time for cohesion to develop/social events;
10. Social cohesion can be an advantage, but not essential.

b. 8 marks *(sub max 1 mark)*:

1. Most appropriate form of training would be interval/fartlek training;

(Mark first training method only)

(Sub max 5 marks)

2. During the short sprints or bursts of activity/0-10metres/2 seconds ATP
   (Do not credit anaerobic);

3. During the 10 – 50/70 metres/up to 10 seconds ATP-PC/alactic system;
4. PC/PC is broken down to release energy/make ATP;
5. During the 70m+/30secs – 2 mins/ lactic acid/lactate anaerobic system/anaerobic glycolysis;
6 During periods of inactivity/walk/jog- aerobic/aerobic glycolysis;
7. Use of aerobic period to restore PC/CP stores/remove lactate;
8. And re-synthesis ATP. *(in order to credit must link to 7)*.

(Sub max 5 marks)

9. Mimics/replicates match running/work pattern;
10. Can combine/alternate periods of work and recovery/equiv;
11. Can change/manipulate/set the intensity of work;
12. By varying distance;
13. Or speed;
14. And frequency/duration of period of work;
15. Can change/manipulate length of recovery period;
16. This allows you to train/stress a particular energy system.

8 marks

Sample Answer (numbers in brackets refer to points on the mark scheme)

a. Cohesion is a group sticking together to achieve a common goal (1). A coach can help a team to become cohesive by team bonding activities such as a day (9) out away from training. They may also set up practices during training (5) so they get to know each others play. A coach may also get the team to complete a task without help from anyone else. They can also make sure each player understands exactly what they have to do to complete their role (7).

b. During a game of hockey all of the energy systems are used at different times.

The aerobic system is used predominantly when jogging and walking (6) around the pitch, due to it being light exercise and oxygen can be used. This helps to remove lactic acid (7) that has built up during the game. The lactic acid system is used for high intensity activities such as longer sprints up and down the pitch when the play goes from one end to the other (5). This system does not use oxygen so it is for fast activities and would be used for activities which last over 30 seconds. During a penalty flick stored ATP would split (2) as the action is over very quickly and gives energy for a short burst of speed. The last system to be used is the ATP-PC system for short sprints up to 30 metres (3).

The most appropriate form of training for the player would be interval training (1) because the game of hockey is made up of short sprints and periods of lower work (9). It is a good method of training because you can vary the distance (12) of the running and the recovery (15) to be like the game itself.

Examiner Comments

a. The answer initially gives the explanation of the term in the question, which is always good practice. The second part of the question requires applied knowledge and practical strategies to develop cohesion. Three different methods are provided, each creditworthy. It may have been advisable to include at least one if not two extra strategies in case those already given were classed as repeat answers or incorrect.

b. The question is sub-divided into two sections and the answer is well structured, approaching each in turn. Each of the energy systems used in a game are identified and a specific example is given. The examiner is able to see that the student has a clear understanding of the relationship between the different systems. The second part identifies correctly the training method which is most appropriate and gives a clear explanation of their reasoning.

This is a typical synoptic question as it covers both psychological and physiological aspects of the course, from AS and A2 components.